THE BiG BOOK
OF **BiG**
LAUGHS
FOR KiDS

OTHER BOOKS
BY SANDY SILVERTHORNE

Crack Yourself Up Jokes for Kids
More Crack Yourself Up Jokes for Kids
Made You Laugh!
Now That's Funny
The Best Worst Dad Jokes
The Big Book of Crack Yourself Up Jokes for Kids
Kids' Big Questions for God

THE BIG BOOK OF BIG LAUGHS FOR KIDS

SANDY SILVERTHORNE

Revell

a division of Baker Publishing Group
Grand Rapids, Michigan

© 2020, 2021 by Sandy Silverthorne

Published by Revell
a division of Baker Publishing Group
Grand Rapids, Michigan
www.revellbooks.com

Combined edition published 2023
ISBN 978-0-8007-4526-4 (paper)
ISBN 978-0-8007-4527-1 (casebound)
ISBN 978-1-4934-4361-1 (ebook)

Previously published in two separate volumes:
Made You Laugh! © 2020
Now That's Funny © 2021

Printed in the United States of America

The author is represented by WordServe Literary Group, www.wordserveliterary.com.

23   24   25   26   27   28   29   7   6   5   4   3   2   1

What goes *dot-dot, dash-dash, squeak-squeak*? A message in Mouse code. Ha! Made you laugh! Want to hear a joke about paper? Never mind, it's tearable. Made you laugh again! Whether you have a quiet little giggle or a side-splitting guffaw, this book is guaranteed to make you laugh. And if it doesn't, you need to have your funny bone examined.

What do you get when you cross a chicken with a robber? A peck-pocket.

This book is filled with hilarious stories, one-liners, riddles, knock-knock jokes, and lots of crazy, silly illustrations. It also has some totally tough tongue twisters to test your tongue-twisting talents. So what are you waiting for? Go for it! Go ahead and make your friends, your brothers and sisters, your teacher, and even your parents laugh! And while you're at it, make yourself laugh too!

MADE YOU LAUGH!

Q: Where do cows go to have fun?

A: To the amooooosement park.

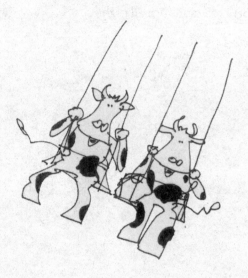

Q: What kind of bee can't make up its mind?

A: A maybee.

Patient: Doctor! I'm convinced I'm a pumpkin. Can you help me?

Psychiatrist: Sure, I think I can carve out some time in my schedule.

Patient: I keep dreaming I'm in a washing machine.

Doctor: Wow! What happens?

Patient: I toss and turn all night.

Q: What has lots of ears but can't hear?

A: A cornfield.

Knock, knock.

Who's there?

Ammonia.

Ammonia who?

Ammonia little kid. What do you expect?

I'm an exchange student.

Q: What do you call a droid who always takes the long way?

A: R2Detour.

Q: How do you make a lemon drop?

A: Just let it fall.

Q: What do you call a duck who gets straight A's?

A: A wise quacker.

Q: How do you talk to a giant?

A: Use big words.

Q: What do you call two birds who are in love?

A: Tweethearts.

Q: How does a scientist keep his breath sweet?

A: With experi-mints.

Sunday School Teacher: Why is it important to be
quiet in church?

Kid: Because people are sleeping?

Teacher: Nick, who invented fractions?

Nick: Henry the 1/8th?

Rowan: I went riding this afternoon.

Remy: Horseback?

Rowan: He sure is. He got back about an hour before
I did.

Q: Where does Pharaoh go for his back pain?

A: To the Cairo-practor.

Reporter: How did you like that new restaurant on Mars?

Astronaut: The food was great, but there wasn't much
atmosphere.

Q: What did the astronaut say when he crashed into the moon?

A: "I Apollo-gize."

Ron: How do pickles enjoy the weekend?

Jon: They relish it.

Bill: What do you call an old snowman?

Phil: Water.

TONGUE TWISTERS

She should shun the shining sun.

Fred threw thirty-three free throws.

Skunks sat on a stump, and the stump stunk.

Mix, miss, mix.

Q: What do you get when you cross a centipede with a parrot?

A: A walkie-talkie.

Ben: How do novels stay warm?

Len: They put on their book jackets.

Aiden: Did you see that cop dressed as a pilot?

Caden: Yeah, I guess he's a plane-clothes officer.

As soon as you find out someone has ten thousand bees, marry them. That's when you know they're a keeper.

Tourist: What's the fastest way to get downtown?

Local: Are you walking or driving?

Tourist: Driving.

Local: That's the fastest way.

When someone tells me to stop acting like a flamingo, that's when I put my foot down.

Knock, knock.

Who's there?

Yule log.

Yule log who?

Yule log the door after I come in, won't you?

If a gang of robbers all jumped into a pool at once, would that be called a crime wave?

CANNONBALL!!!!

Al: I told my boss that three companies were after me and I needed a raise.

Sal: What companies?

Al: Gas, water, and electric.

My uncle used to be a banker, but then he lost interest.

Q: What goes *ha, ha, ha, plop?*
A: Someone laughing their head off.

Q: What did the beaver say to the tree?
A: "It's been nice gnawing you."

Q: What's the difference between your elbow and a rabbit's cell phone?
A: One's a funny bone, and the other's a bunny's phone.

Jenny: How do porcupines play leapfrog?
Benny: Very carefully.

Q: What do you get when you cross a porcupine with a balloon?

A: POP!

Bill: How do chickens dance?

Jill: Chick to chick.

Hannah: What goes *dot-dot, dash-dash, squeak-squeak*?

Anna: A message in Mouse code.

Dot-dot dash-dash
squeak-squeak

Q: What do you call a pan flying through space?

A: An Unidentified Frying Object.

Iris: Why did the astronaut bring scissors, paper, string, and glue on his trip?

Bo: He wanted to do spacecrafts.

Q: What's an astronaut's favorite beverage?

A: Gravi-tea.

Q: How do you make a baby go to sleep in space?

A: You rocket.

Q: What's a cow's favorite party game?

A: Mooo-sical chairs.

It was a terrible summer for Humpty Dumpty, but he had a great fall.

Len: What did the bankrupt cat say?

Ben: "I'm paw."

Mike: Which nail does a carpenter hate to hit?

Ike: His thumbnail.

Joe: Why was the archaeologist upset?

Bo: Because his career was in ruins.

Ron: How many magicians does it take to change a light bulb?

Don: Only one, but he changes it into a rabbit.

Q: Where do geologists like to spend their time?

A: At rock festivals.

Terry: Why did the bank teller stand right next to the vault?

Jerry: He wanted to be on the safe side.

Joe: My dad gets paid for making faces.

Flo: Wow! Where does he work?

Joe: In a clock factory.

Ed: Why don't hot dogs act in the movies?

Ned: The rolls are never good enough.

Q: What's a tree's favorite drink?

A: Root beer.

Chloe: What's tall, French, and delicious?

Kylie: The Trifle Tower.

Q: What did the scissors say to the hair?

A: "It won't be long now."

Q: What's a frog's favorite year?

A: Leap year.

Q: What's green, hops, and can be heard for miles?

A: A froghorn.

Knock, knock.

Who's there?

House.

House who?

House it going?

Knock, knock.

Who's there?

Alaska.

Alaska who?

Alaska only once. Open the door!

Knock, knock.

Who's there?

Wooden shoe.

Wooden shoe who?

Wooden shoe like to know?

Mason: Why did Sammy run past his classroom?

Jason: He wanted to pass his test.

Randy: Why did the teacher wear sunglasses in her classroom?

Andy: Because all of her students were so bright.

Camper: How do you know that's a dogwood tree?

Ranger: I can tell by its bark.

Q: What illness can a plane catch?

A: The flew.

Ron: What was the spider doing on the computer?

Don: Designing a website.

Peg: What do you get when you cross detergent with a composer?

Meg: A soap opera.

A guy went to a home improvement store.

"Yeah, I'd like to buy some boards," he said.

"How long would you like them?" the worker asked.

"Oh," he said, "a long time. I'm building a house."

Knock, knock.

Who's there?

A door.

A door who?

Adorable me—that's who!

Knock, knock.

Who's there?

Oscar.

Oscar who?

Oscar if she can come out and play.

Knock, knock.

Who's there?

Henrietta.

Henrietta who?

Henrietta whole pizza by himself.

Want to hear a joke about paper? Never mind, it's tearable.

Q: How does a penguin build his house?
A: Igloos it together.

Teacher: Christy, please spell *wrong*.
Christy: R-O-N-G.
Teacher: That's wrong.
Christy: Isn't that what you wanted?

Teacher: Jenny, can you tell me where the English Channel is?

Jenny: I can't. We don't have cable.

Ben: Why couldn't the bicycle stand up by itself?

Len: It was two-tired.

I wouldn't buy anything made with Velcro. It's a total rip-off.

Asher: I've come up with a groundbreaking invention!

Bo: What do you call it?

Asher: A shovel.

5/4 of people admit they're bad with fractions.

Jenny: I'm thinking of going on an all-almond diet.

Benny: That's just nuts!

Knock, knock.

Who's there?

Annie.

Annie who?

Annie body home?

Knock, knock.

Who's there?

Al.

Al who?

Al give you a kiss if you open this door.

Q: What spends all its time on the floor but never gets dirty?

A: Your shadow.

Q: What animal needs to wear a wig?

A: A bald eagle.

Q: Where do fish keep their money?

A: In the riverbank.

Len: I'm taking up rock collecting.

Ben: How's it going?

Len: I'm picking it up as I go along.

Jill: Why did the kids bring honey to the teacher?

Will: Because they were all bee students.

Q: What do you call a flower that runs on electricity?

A: A power plant.

Q: Why did the dog get all A's in class?

A: Because he was the teacher's pet.

Q: What do you call a shoe made out of a banana?

A: A slipper.

Iris: What's a skeleton's favorite musical instrument?

Harper: A trombone.

Q: How do billboards talk to one another?

A: Sign language.

Peg: Did you hear about the bedbug that was expecting?

Meg: Yeah, she's going to have her baby in the spring.

Q: How did the farmer meet his wife?

A: He tractor down.

Q: How do astronauts keep clean?

A: They take meteor showers.

Ava: Why are you taking your computer to the shoe store?

Fred: It needs to be rebooted.

Chad: Why did the café hire the pig?

Rad: He was really good at bacon.

Give me a shingle with a shimmy and a shake!

Q: What did the hot dog say when he crossed the finish line?

A: "Hooray! I'm a wiener!"

Jill: What kind of car does Mickey Mouse's girlfriend drive?

Phil: A Minnie van.

Q: What's a little bear's favorite dessert?

A: Cub cakes.

Rowan: Why shouldn't you tell a joke while you're standing on ice?

Ava: Because it might crack up.

Jim: What did the barber say to the bee?

Tim: "Do you want a buzz cut?"

Jeremiah: Last night I dreamed I was a car muffler.

Brooks: Wow! What happened?

Jeremiah: I woke up exhausted.

People are usually shocked when they find out I'm not a very good electrician.

Peg: Where do you learn how to make banana splits?

Meg: At Sundae school.

Rancher: Where do cows buy their clothes?

Farmer: From cattle-logs.

If you take your watch to get fixed, don't pay the guy before; wait till the time is right.

Q: What do you call a snake wearing a hard hat?

A: A boa constructor.

My friend borrowed my grandfather clock. Now he owes me big time.

What's yours is hours.

Chloe: My mom turned thirty-two yesterday and had a really short party.

Kylie: Why?

Chloe: It was her thirty-second birthday.

Not only is this new thesaurus terrible, it's also terrible.

Ed: The ducks keep trying to bite my dog.

Ned: Why?

Ed: He's a pure bread.

Q: What did one firefly say to the other?

A: "You glow, girl!"

Q: Where do chickens like to eat?

A: At a roosterant.

Q: What does a girl spider wear when she gets married?

A: A webbing dress.

Q: I have lots of keys, but I can't open any door. What am I?

A: A piano.

Thanks for explaining the word *many* for me. It means a lot.

Jay: What did the penny say to his penny friends?

Ray: "We make a lot of cents!"

Q: Why did the spider buy a new car?

A: 'Cause he wanted to take it out for a spin.

Q: What do you call a potato wearing glasses?

A: A spec-tater.

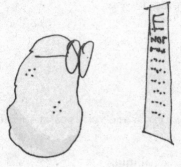

Christy: Why does a grape make a great mom?

Misty: Why?

Christy: Because she loves raisin' children.

Lonny: What do you get when you cross a parrot with a gorilla?

Donny: I don't know, but whatever he says, you'd better listen.

Ed: What do you get when you cross a flower with Lassie?

Ned: A collie-flower.

Q: What do you get when you cross a sprinter with a dog?

A: A 100-yard dachshund.

Q: Why don't banks allow kangaroos to open accounts?

A: Their checks always bounce.

Two kids were looking at the night sky.

Connor: Wow! Is that Venus or Neptune?

Deagan: I don't know. I'm not from around here.

Q: Where do sheep go after high school?

A: To the ewe-niversity.

Q: What did the duck say to the class clown?

A: "You quack me up!"

Q: What's a pig's favorite ballet?

A: *Swine Lake.*

Jill: Did you hear the story about the peacock?

Phil: No, but I heard it was a beautiful tale.

Q: What do you get when you cross a reptile with a duck?

A: A quack-o-dile.

I entered the suntan Olympics, but I only got bronze.

City Guy: Is chicken soup good for your health?

Farmer: Not if you're the chicken.

Q: What do you get if a hen lays an egg on the top of a hill?

A: Egg rolls.

Oops.

Teacher: I want to discuss your son's appearance.

Parent: What about it?

Teacher: He hasn't made one in this classroom since September.

Isabel: Why do you have that rubber band around your head?

Charlotte: I'm trying to make snap decisions.

Jill: What are you reading?

Phil: I don't know.

Jill: But you were reading out loud.

Phil: I know, but I wasn't listening.

Diner: I'll have the steak, and make it lean.

Waiter: Yes, sir. To the right or the left?

TONGUE TWiSTERS

Tragedy, strategy.

Cinnamon, aluminum, linoleum.

A slimy snake slithered through the sandy Sahara.

So this is the sushi chef.

How can a clam cram in a clean clam can?

Teacher: Jimmy, do you need a pencil?

Jimmy: Yeah. I ain't got one.

Teacher: Jimmy, where's your grammar?

Jimmy: She's at home, but she ain't got no pencil either.

Doctor: Can you breathe in and out for me three times?

Patient: Are you checking my lungs?

Doctor: No, I need to clean my glasses.

Teacher: Why did Robin Hood only rob from the rich?

Kid: 'Cause the poor didn't have any money.

Q: Where do hamsters go on vacation?

A: Hamsterdam.

Asher: What do you call it when five hundred stamps escape from the post office and run down the street?

Harper: A stampede!

Q: What can you hold in your right hand but not in your left hand?

A: Your left elbow.

Q: What fish performs operations at the fish clinic?

A: The sturgeon.

Hello, I'm Dr. Bass.
I'll be your sturgeon.

Woman: Doctor, I keep getting smaller!

Doctor: Well, I guess you'll have to be a little patient.

I gave all my dead batteries away today. Free of charge.

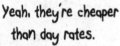

Jim: I'm going to become a candlemaker. It's so easy.

Tim: What do you mean?

Jim: They only work on wick ends.

I broke my finger last week. On the other hand, I'm okay.

Q: Where do pigs go when they're sick?

A: To the hogs-pital.

Max: Why can't sheep drive a car?

Alsea: 'Cause they can only make ewe-turns.

Q: What's a dog's favorite snack?

A: Mutt-zerella cheese.

Terry: I bought a drum for my cat.

Jerry: Why's that?

Terry: She's a purr-cussionist.

Joe: How do you keep a rattlesnake from striking?

Moe: Pay him a decent wage.

Phil: Why aren't koala bears considered real bears?

Bill: They don't meet the koala-fications.

Never criticize anyone till you've walked a mile in their shoes. That way, when you do criticize them, you're a mile away and you have their shoes.

I'm terrified of elevators, so I'm taking steps to avoid them.

Q: What do snowmen eat for breakfast?

A: Frosted Flakes.

An older couple was driving through Wenatchee, Washington, on a vacation. They kept arguing about how to pronounce the name of the town. When they stopped at a fast-food place, the man went to the counter and asked if the worker would pronounce where they were, real slowly. The worker responded by saying, "Buuuurrrrgeerrr Kiiiinngggggg."

Every time I see an autobiography on the bookshelf, I just skip to the "About the Author" section to save time.

Dan: I just got some pills from the doctor for my sleeping problem.

Jan: So why do you look so unhappy?

Dan: You have to take one every thirty minutes!

Q: Why can't the Three Bears get into their house?

A: 'Cause Goldilocks the door.

Q: What's a lawyer's favorite food?

A: Sue-shi.

Q: What do you get when you cross a small bear with a French dog?

A: Winnie the Poodle.

Mom: Why do you make so much noise when you eat your cereal?

Kid: Teacher said we should always start our day with a sound breakfast.

I went shopping on an empty stomach yesterday. Now I'm the happy owner of Aisle 7.

At my last job interview, the manager said he was looking for someone responsible. I told him that whenever anything went wrong at my last job, they always said I was responsible.

Adam and Eve were talking one afternoon in the Garden of Eden.

Eve: Do you really love me, Adam?

Adam: Who else?

Terry: Where do fish sleep?

Jerry: In the riverbed.

I got in trouble yesterday at customs. They said, "Papers?" And I said "Scissors!"

Mom: Aiden, did you do your chores?

Aiden: Yes, Mom, I just polished off a chocolate bar.

Dentist: You need a crown.

Patient: Finally, someone who understands me.

Q: How do you make a hot dog stand?

A: Take away its chair.

Q: What does a snail say when he's riding on a turtle's back?

A: "Wheeee!"

Mom: Where's your report card, Sam?

Sam: I loaned it to Jaxon.

Mom: Why?

Sam: So he could scare his parents.

Sal: Why did the watchmaker go to the doctor?

Hal: He was all wound up.

Q: What's worse than a giraffe with a sore throat?

A: A centipede with athlete's foot.

Rick: My kid is afraid of Santa Claus.

Nick: Oh, Claustrophobic, huh?

Kylie: Have you ever seen a fishbowl?

Iris: No, but I've seen a cowhide.

Terry: What's a soccer player's favorite color?

Jerry: Solid gooooaaaalllllld!

Always buy a thermometer during the winter. Because during the summer they go up.

Teacher: How many feet in a yard?

Kid: It depends on how many people are standing in it.

Fred: Who was on the phone?

Remy: I don't know. They said it's long distance from Hong Kong. I said, "It sure is," and hung up.

Teacher: Lucas, please use the word *fascinate* in a sentence.

Lucas: My jacket has ten buttons, but I can only fascinate.

Teacher: Who can tell me what a *myth* is?

Connor: A female moth?

Q: What do elves do after school?

A: Their gnome-work.

Teacher: Who leads all the orcas?

Deagan: The Prince of Wales?

Come on, everyone! Follow me!

Hannah: If we breathe oxygen during the day, what do we breathe at night?

Chloe: Nitrogen?

Sal: What's the hardest thing about falling out of bed?

Al: The floor.

Alsea: Why do you have an egg in your bed?

Caden: 'Cause I want to get up at the crack of dawn.

Q: Why was the wisdom tooth all dressed up?

A: Because the dentist was taking her out that night.

My brother borrowed my bike. I told him to treat it as if it were his own. So he sold it.

Dan: What do you get when you cross a tiger with a lamb?

Jan: A striped sweater.

Q: What did the astronaut say in a press conference?
A: "No comet."

Knock, knock.

Who's there?

Champ.

Champ who?

Champoo the dog. He's really muddy.

Q: How did the explorer discover the glacier?

A: He had good ice sight.

Did you hear about the auto mechanic who was ready to re-tire?

Let's hit the road.

Swimmer: Hey, every time I go scuba diving, I hear music.

Lifeguard: Oh, it must be a coral group.

Patient: Are you the head doctor?

Jim: No, I'm the foot doctor.

Q: What do you call a one-hundred-year-old ant?

A: An antique.

Q: Why was the centipede late for school?

A: He was playing "This Little Piggy" with his brother.

Q: How did the beetle find out all the caterpillar's secrets?

A: He bugged his phone.

Kate: What do you call an ant who's good with numbers?

Nate: An accountant.

Q: What did one light bulb say to the other?

A: "Let's go out tonight."

Q: What do you get when you cross peanut butter with a quilt?

A: A bread spread.

Q: Where does a shrimp do his shopping?

A: At a prawn shop.

Q: When is a boat not a boat?

A: When it's afloat.

Isabel: Why couldn't the bee go to the dance?

Charlotte: 'Cause it was a mothball.

Chad: Where do bees eat lunch?

Rad: At the bee-stro.

Dan: Why are you dancing with that jar?

Fran: It says, "To open, twist."

Q: What's a polar bear's favorite writing utensil?

A: A ballpoint penguin.

Q: What wise bird hangs out in the bathroom?

A: A hoo-towel.

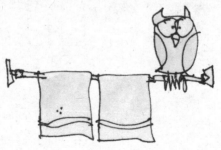

Q: Where do fish get clean?

A: In their bass tub.

Roommate #1: What's the best way to keep your hair dry in the shower?

Roommate #2: Don't turn on the water.

Susannah: What do you call someone who sees a crime in the rain?

Rose: An eye-wetness.

Q: What do you call a dog who's really dirty and needs a bath?

A: A germy shepherd.

Len: Why did the policeman always carry a bar of soap with him?

Ben: Because he worked in a city with a high grime rate.

Q: What do you call a six-pack of ducks?

A: A box of quackers.

Q: What's a bumblebee's favorite music?

A: Bee-bop.

Q: What kind of opera star sings in the shower?

A: A soap-rano.

Q: How can you tell when you're in a snake family's bathroom?

A: The towels say *Hiss* and *Hers*.

Rose: Why are you standing in front of the mirror with your eyes closed?

Rowan: I want to see what I look like when I'm asleep.

Teacher: Max, use the word *diploma* in a sentence.

Max: When da sink's stopped up, we call diploma.

Harper: I'd like to donate my aquarium to the army.

Asher: Why would they want that?

Harper: I heard they needed more tanks.

TONGUE TWiSTERS

If Stu chews shoes, should Stu choose the shoes he chews?

Pirates' private property.

Three short sword sheaths.

On a lazy laser razor lies a laser ray eraser.

Phil: Why did the plumber quit work early yesterday?

Bill: He was drained.

Peg: I stopped dating the chiropractor.

Meg: Why was that?

Peg: I got tired of all his back talk.

Why do you have that shoe up to your ear?!?

I'm listening to sole music.

Q: What did the pirate get on his math test?

A: Sea plus.

Q: What do you get when you cross a pig with an evergreen tree?

A: A porky-pine.

Q: How does a lifeguard get to work?

A: He carpools.

Q: What does the germ wear when he gets up in the morning?

A: His little microbe.

Iris: Why are you wearing that Zorro cape to bed?

Bo: I'm trying to catch some Zs.

Jess: What does a chimney sweep carry with him at all times?

Fess: His soot-case.

Harper: Why did you invite that baseball player to go camping with us?

Asher: I needed someone to pitch the tent.

Remy: Why is Sir Lancelot always so tired?

Isabel: 'Cause he works the knight shift.

I turned vegan, but I think it's a big missed steak.

Did you hear about the little old woman who lived in a sock? Her shoe was being soled.

Q: What do bakers read to their kids at night?

A: Bread-time stories.

Q: What do you get when you cross a dentist with a boat?

A: A tooth ferry.

Q: Where does Santa stay when he's on vacation?

A: At a ho, ho, hotel.

Q: What's a cow's favorite night?

A: One with a full mooooon.

Braeden: What can dunk, knows how to dribble, and is three and a half feet tall?

Caden: A seven-foot basketball player taking a bow.

Q: What do you get when you cross a sheep with a monkey?

A: A baa-boon.

Mike: What do you get when you cross an elephant with a kangaroo?

Ike: Great big holes all over the jungle.

Q: Where do giraffes go to learn?

A: High school.

Dog: Hey, Cow, what are you doing?

Cow: Shhh, I'm on a steak-out.

When fish are in schools, they sometimes take debate.

Connor: Did you hear about the dry cleaner who was always late?

Chloe: Yeah, he was pressed for time.

Man: Sorry I'm late; I just got here. I'm sick.

Doctor: Flu?

Man: No, I took a bus.

Mom: Don't you ever let me catch you doing that again!

Kid: I'll try, but you're so quiet sometimes.

Q: What do you get when you cross Christmas with St. Patrick's Day?

A: St. O'Claus.

Bill: Why are you wearing that wet suit?

Jill: I'm going to a wedding shower.

Q: What's a duck's favorite part of the Constitution?

A: The Bill of Rights.

Q: What did the lumberjack do after he cut down the tree?

A: He took a bough.

BACKWARD JOKES

Backward jokes give the answer first, then the question. Here's an example:

Answer: UCLA.

Question: What happens when the smog clears in Southern California?

Get the idea? So, go ahead and check these out:

Answer: 7 Up.

Question: What happens at Snow White's house when the alarm clock goes off?

Okay, everybody, time to get up!

Answer: Dr Pepper.

Question: Who married Nurse Salt?

Answer: In a class by himself.

Question: How do you describe an only child who's homeschooled?

Answer: Descent.

Question: What's the difference between a cat and a skunk?

Answer: Doe-si-doe.

Question: What do you call two deer at a square dance?

Answer: Mississippi.

Question: What do you call a hippie's wife?

Answer: Satellite.

Question: What does the cowboy use to see after dark?

Answer: Ranch dressing.

Question: What do you call it when you wear cowboy clothes?

Answer: Laughingstock.

Question: What do you call cows with a good sense of humor?

Answer: Modem.

Question: What did the landscaper do to the lawns?

Answer: Analog.

Question: What does Ana throw into the fire?

Lonny: I don't trust stairs.

Donny: Why not?

Lonny: They're always up to something.

Ed: Which dogs bark more, young or old?

Ned: It's about arf and arf.

Q: How did pioneer puppies get out West?

A: They traveled in waggin' trains.

Q: What do you get when you cross a turtle with a boomerang?

A: Snappy comebacks.

Q: How did the cows get away from Farmer Brown's farm?

A: They used a mooooving van.

Q: How did the lambs get to the moon?

A: By space-sheep.

Why do people say "tuna fish" when they don't say "beef mammal" or "chicken bird"?

Q: What does a snake give its babies before bed?

A: Hugs and hisses.

Donny: What do you call a bunch of little dogs with cameras?

Lonny: Pup-arazzi.

Q: What do you get when you cross a pouting child with a rhino?

A: A whine-oceros.

I'm hungry, when do we eat?
Why's it so hot in here? Turn on the
air conditioning! Why do we have to
wait so long?

Deagan: Why are you ironing that four-leaf clover?

Hannah: I'm trying to press my luck.

Q: Who leaps over tall buildings in order to wake people up?

A: Clock Kent.

Q: What do you call a flock of sheep rolling down a hill?

A: A lamb-slide.

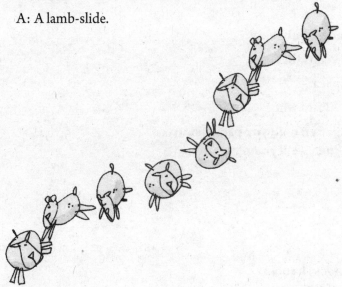

Brian: Why do pirates have such a hard time learning the alphabet?

Ryan: Because they sometimes get stuck at C for years. And then they get caught at *AAAARRRRRR*.

Knock, knock.

Who's there?

Baby owl.

Baby owl who?

Baby owl see you when you open the door.

Knock, knock.

Who's there?

Alpaca.

Alpaca who?

**Alpaca trunk, you pack a suitcase,
then we'll go on vacation.**

Knock, knock.

Who's there?

Colleen.

Colleen who?

Colleen up this mess out here.

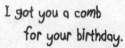

I got you a comb
for your birthday.

Wow, thanks. I'll never part with it.

Q: **What do you get when you cross a chicken with a skunk?**

A: A fowl smell.

Have you heard the rumor about the peanut butter? I'd better not tell you; it might spread.

Q: **Why couldn't the lamb get up in time?**

A: He was still a sheep.

Q: **What happens when you cross a painter with a police officer?**

A: You have a brush with the law.

Q: **What do snowmen do on the weekend?**

A: They chill out.

Q: Why did the boy study in the hot air balloon?

A: He wanted to get a higher education.

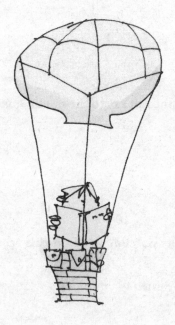

Q: What do you call a group of singing dinosaurs?

A: A tyranno-chorus.

So, I was washing my car with my friend when he asked, "Why can't you just use a sponge?"

Q: Why did the boy sprinkle sugar on his pillow?

A: He wanted to have sweet dreams.

Q: What did one nut say to the nut he was chasing?

A: "I'm gonna cashew!"

Q: Why did the watchmaker enjoy his vacation so much?

A: He finally learned to unwind.

Jay: What does the Dentist of the Year receive?

Ray: A little plaque.

Q: Who is Santa's favorite singer?
A: Elfis Presley.

Ron: What do dentists call their dental X-rays?
John: Tooth pics.

Q: What city can never stay put?
A: Rome.

Q: What do you call a lazy kangaroo?
A: A pouch potato.

Q: What do you call a cinnamon bun who's at the top of the class?

A: An honor roll.

Iris: Did you see the angry pancake?

Bo: Yeah, he's ready to flip.

To be Frank, I'd have to change my name.

Joe: How does the shark from *Jaws* like his breakfast eggs?

Flo: Terri-fried!

Q: How do leaves travel around?

A: By autumn-mobile.

I have a fear of speed bumps, but I'm slowly getting over it.

Ava: Did you hear about the frog that got a job at a hotel?

Susannah: Really? What job?

Ava: He's a bellhop.

I need you to take these to room 407 and hop to it!

Q: What plants do chickens grow on?

A: Eggplants.

Peg: What colors would you paint the sun and the wind?

Meg: I'd paint the sun rose and the wind blue.

Knock, knock.

Who's there?

Juno.

Juno who?

Juno I'm out here, right?

Knock, knock.

Who's there?

Yacht.

Yacht who?

Yacht to know by now.

TONGUE TWISTERS

Two tiny tigers took two taxis to town.

Dust is a disk's worst enemy.

She sees cheese.

Crush grapes, grapes crush, crush grapes.

Q: What's the richest kind of air?

A: Billionaire.

If you have any good fish puns, let minnow.

Q: What do you call a rabbit who's really cool?

A: A hip-hopper.

Q: What kind of driver never uses a car?

A: A screwdriver.

Q: What do you call a dinosaur who's always on time?

A: A pronto-saurus.

Sorry I'm late.

Jim: What did the carpet say to the floor?

Tim: "Don't worry, I got you covered."

Knock, knock.

Who's there?

Albie.

Albie who?

Albie out here if you need me.

Q: How do cats decorate their houses?

A: With fur-niture.

Teacher: Sandy, name six wild animals.

Sandy: Two lions and four tigers.

Teacher: Are you chewing gum?

Jamie: No, ma'am, I'm Jamie Thompson.

Principal: Jackson, what time do you wake up in the morning?

Jackson: About an hour and a half after I get to school.

I just wrote a book on reverse psychology. Do *not* read it.

The other day my wife asked me to pass her the lipstick, and I accidentally passed her a glue stick instead. She still isn't talking to me.

Q: What sound does a chicken's phone make?

A: *Wing, wing.*

Q: What kind of dog lives at the North Pole?

A: A chili dog.

Q: What do you call a group of friends making a sweater?

A: Social knit-working.

Q: What's a little bear's favorite side dish?

A: Corn on the cub.

Mason: Did you hear about the dog who chased a stick for five miles?

Jason: That's pretty far-fetched.

Teacher: Why are you crawling into my classroom?

Max: Because you said, "Don't anyone dare walk in late!"

Teacher: Maddie, you copied Christy's paper, didn't you?

Maddie: How did you know?

Teacher: Well, for one, an answer on Christy's paper says, "I don't know," and yours says, "Me neither."

Dad: Matthew, this says you're at the bottom of your class of twenty. That's terrible!

Matthew: It could be worse.

Dad: How?

Matthew: It could have been a bigger class.

Jon: What are you doing, Ron?

Ron: Writing a letter to myself.

Jon: What does it say?

Ron: I don't know; I won't get it till tomorrow.

Teacher: Jon, how many *i*'s do you use to spell *Mississippi*?

Jon: None. I can do it blindfolded.

Teacher: What's your name, young man?

Kid: Henry.

Teacher: Excuse me, you need to say *sir*!

Kid: Okay. Sir Henry.

I love elevator jokes. They work on so many levels.

Teacher: I'm happy to give you a 70 in science.

Bo: Why don't you really enjoy yourself and give me a 100?

Asher: I can't go to school today; I don't feel well.

 Mom: Where don't you feel well?

Asher: In school.

The brain is an amazing instrument. It starts working the minute you wake up in the morning, and it never stops until you're called on in class.

Diner: Waiter, what is this fly doing in my soup?

Waiter: Looks like the Macarena.

These shoes will be tight for the next two weeks.

Okay, I'll start wearing them the third week.

Kylie makes a phone call to her aunt's house.

Kylie: Hi, may I speak to Jonah please?

Aunt: Why, Jonah's only a baby. He hasn't learned to talk yet.

Kylie: That's okay. I'll hold.

Little Girl: How much are these diapers?

Clerk: Nine dollars plus tax.

Little Girl: Oh, that's okay. We don't need the tacks; my mom uses safety pins.

Al: Is your sister spoiled?

Sal: No, that's just the perfume she wears.

A woman was walking down the street one afternoon when she saw a small boy trying to reach the doorbell of a nearby house. Sensing his frustration, she walked up on the porch and pushed the doorbell for him. Then she turned to him and said, "What do we do now, young man?"

"Run!" he said, and he took off.

Charlotte: How did the mice do in school?

Susannah: They just squeaked by.

Lawyer: Why is the judge sending for the locksmith?

Bailiff: Oh, the key witness is missing.

Q: What's 5,700 feet tall and has four heads?

A: Mount Rushmore.

Q: What's a frog's favorite musical instrument?

A: A hop-sichord.

A clown held the door open for me this morning. I thought it was a nice jester.

I asked the lion in my wardrobe what he was doing there. He said, "Narnia business."

Q: Why did the pie go to the dentist?

A: To get a filling.

Q: What kind of bird works at a construction site?

A: A crane.

Q: What do you call an alligator who's a thief?

A: A crookodile.

Q: Why did the tree surgeon open another office?

A: He was branching out.

Couldn't figure out how to work my seat belt. Then it clicked.

Judge: The charge is stealing a blanket. How do you
plead?

Defendant: Not quilty.

Q: What's Santa's favorite sandwich?

A: Peanut butter and jolly.

Q: Where do penguins keep their money?

A: In snowbanks.

Talk about cold cash.

Terry: Why was the swim instructor fired?

Jerry: He kept people wading too long.

Q: What is gray, weighs three tons, and soars through the air?

A: A hippo on a hang glider.

Q: What did the skeleton order at the restaurant?
A: Spare ribs.

Customer: May I have a pair of alligator shoes, please?
Shoe Salesperson: Certainly. What size is your alligator?

Q: Where do you go to weigh a whale?
A: To the whale-weigh station.

Teacher: Max, describe a synonym.
Max: It's a word you use when you can't spell the
other word.

Teacher: Tyler, what comes before March?
Tyler: Forward!

Teacher: Did your father help you on this assignment?

Caden: Nope, he did it all on his own.

Man: I've been riding this bus to work for fifteen years now.

Lady: Oh my goodness, where did you get on?

Donny: The trombone player lost his job in the band.

Lonny: Why?

Donny: He just kept letting things slide.

Stan: Is this a good lake for fish?

Dan: It must be; I can't get any of them to come out.

A little boy swallowed a quarter and two dimes. When his mom took him to the doctor, they took an X-ray.

"I think he's going to be fine," the doctor said as he looked at the picture.

"Why do you say that?" the mom asked.

"I don't see any change in him," the doctor answered.

Reporter: Congratulations! You actually cloned yourself! How do you feel?

Scientist: I'm beside myself!

Teacher: Harper, use the word *folder* in a sentence.

Harper: We need to show respect folder people.

A deer, a skunk, and a duck were at a diner. When the check came, the deer had no doe and the skunk didn't have a scent, so the duck said, "Put it on my bill."

Al: I don't have a cent to my name.

Sal: Are you going to get a job?

Al: No, I'm gonna change my name.

Max: I put five dollars in the change machine.

Alsea: What happened?

Max: Would you believe it? I'm still me.

Mrs. Taylor: Doctor, my husband is convinced he's a boomerang.

Doctor: Don't worry, he'll come around.

TONGUE TWISTERS

Busy buzzing bumblebees.

No need to light a night-light on a light night like tonight.

Many an anemone sees an enemy anemone.

Lesser leather never weathered wetter weather better.

I've made my lawn chicken-proof. Now it's impeccable.

Dan: Rats! I left my watch back there on top of the hill.

Jan: Should you go get it?

Dan: No, it'll run down by itself.

Ryan: Everyone says I got my good looks from my father.

Brian: Oh, is he a plastic surgeon?

Mom: Liam, there were two cookies in the jar last night, and now there is only one. Can you explain that?

Liam: Yeah, it was so dark I missed it.

Jon: Mom, I won the election for class president!

Mom: Honestly?

Jon: Did you have to bring that up?

Q: What do you get when you cross a chicken with a robber?

A: A peck-pocket.

Why are you staring at that can
of frozen orange juice?

The label says, "Concentrate."

Q: What's long and orange and flies at the speed of sound?

A: A jet-propelled carrot.

Teacher: If you received ten dollars from ten people, what would you get?

Jamie: A new bike!

Teacher: What birds do you find in Portugal?

Kid: Portu-geese!

Principal: Do you know a kid named Alex?

Kid: Yup, he sleeps right next to me in geometry.

Teacher: What do you call the little rivers that feed into the Nile?

Kid: Juvi-Niles!

Knock, knock.

Who's there?

Aubrey.

Aubrey who?

Aubrey quiet!

Knock, knock.

Who's there?

Ivan.

Ivan who?

Ivan idea you know who this is.

A lady is sitting on the train as it creeps through the countryside. Finally, she finds the conductor.

  Lady: This is the slowest train I've ever been on. Can't you run any faster?

 Conductor: Sure, but they make me stay on the train.

EMILY BIDDLE'S LITTLE-KNOWN BOOK TITLES

Librarian Emily Biddle has a collection of unusual books in her bookmobile.

Book Titles

Building an Igloo by S. K. Moe

Keep Things Oiled by Russ T. Gates

I Hate the Daytime by Gladys Knight

I Didn't Do It! by Ivan Alibi

A Spring Shower by Wayne Dwops

Tiny Fish by Ann Chovie

Stop Arguing by Xavier Breath

Off to Market by Tobias A. Pig

The New Floor by Lynn O'Leum

House Construction by Bill Jerome Holme

More Book Titles

Discover Chicago by D. Wendy City

You've Got to Be Kidding! by Shirley U. Jest

Why Wait? Let's Go! by Igor Beaver

Keep Your House Clean by Lotta Dust

Come on In! by Doris Open

Winning the Race by Vic Tree

Hot Dog! by Frank Furter

Exploring the Backwoods by Dusty Rhoads

Dress Like the 70s by Polly Esther

Learn Fractions by Lois Denominator

NOW THAT'S FUNNY

Q: **What do you call a hen who can count her own eggs?**

A: A mathemachicken.

Q: **What do you call George Washington's false teeth?**

A: Presidentures.

Q: **What's the coldest tropical island?**

A: Brrr-muda.

Dan: Where did Noah keep the old bees?

Jan: In the ark-hives.

Misty: What kind of bull is the cutest?

Christy: A dor-a-bull.

Logan: What do you get when you cross a police dog
with a skunk?

Rogan: Law and odor.

Q: Why did the silly guy put a fir tree in his living room?

A: He wanted to spruce up the place.

Q: How do you make a strawberry shake?

A: Take it to a scary movie.

Q: What do you call a grumpy cow?

A: Mooo-dy.

TONGUE TWiSTERS

Randy's lawn rake rarely rakes really right.

I saw Susie sitting in a shoeshine shop.

A skunk sat on a stump and thunk the stump stunk, but the stump thunk the skunk stunk.

Background, background, black, black, brown, brown.

Near an ear, a nearer ear, a nearly eerie ear.

Jack: How does the man in the moon hold up his pants?

Zach: With an asteroid belt.

Mason: What do you call a GPS on a battleship?

Jason: A Navy-gator.

Donny: What do you call a pirate who skips classes?

Lonny: Captain Hooky.

Optometrist: Your results aren't very good.

Patient: Can I see them?

Optometrist: Probably not.

The butcher couldn't reach the meat on the top shelf. Apparently, the steaks were too high.

Ted: What kind of cats like to go bowling?

Ed: Alley cats.

Terry: What is Kate's clone's name?

Jerry: Dupli-Kate.

Rowan: What did the speaker at the gardening convention say to the audience?

Ava: "Please be seeded."

Knock, knock.

Who's there?

Cousin.

Cousin who?

**Cousin stead of opening the door,
you're making me stand here.**

**Q: What should you take on a journey through the
desert?**

A: A thirst-aid kit.

Sal: What do you call it when you eat a banana
sundae really fast?

Hal: Lickety-split.

Q: Where can you find a snowman's website?

A: On the winternet.

Q: What sports are trains good at?

A: Track events.

Asher: What would you do if a rhino came at you at 60
miles an hour?

Connor: I'd do 70 miles an hour!

Alsea: Why are you giving your bees away?

Max: They're free-bees!

Knock, knock.

Who's there?

Venice.

Venice who?

Venice this door going to open?

Isabel: How do you get rid of a boomerang?

Rose: You throw it down a one-way street.

Knock, knock.

Who's there?

Isaiah.

Isaiah who?

Isaiah nothing until you open this door.

Knock, knock.

Who's there?

General Lee.

General Lee who?

General Lee, I don't tell knock-knock jokes.

Joe: Don't ever share secrets in a garden.

Flo: Why not?

Joe: Because the potatoes have eyes, the corn has ears, and the beanstalk.

Don't tell anyone, but . . .

Knock, knock.

Who's there?

Danielle.

Danielle who?

Danielle at me; it's not my fault!

Knock, knock.

Who's there?

Jewell.

Jewell who?

Jewell be sorry if you don't open the door!

Knock, knock.

Who's there?

Formosa.

Formosa who?

Formosa the summer, I was away on vacation.

Knock, knock.

Who's there?

Butcher.

Butcher who?

Butcher little arms around me and give me a hug.

Knock, knock.

Who's there?

Heidi.

Heidi who?

Heidi food; a bear's coming!

Chloe: What's big and gray and goes up and down?

Kylie: An elephant on a pogo stick.

Q: What kind of trucks do sheep drive?

A: Ewe-Hauls.

Q: What time is it when you go to the dentist?
A: Tooth-hurty.

Sal: Did you see today's paper?
Hal: No, what's in it?
Sal: My lunch!

Rowan: How do vegetables say goodbye?
Ava: "Peas out."

Q: What do you call a police officer's uniform?
A: A lawsuit.

Q: How do you know when the moon is going broke?

A: When it's down to its last quarter.

Q: What kind of stories do pigs tell their kids at bedtime?

A: Pig-tales.

Q: Why was the mother firefly unhappy?
A: 'Cause her kids weren't very bright.

A guy just threw milk at me. How dairy!

Bill: Why did the wagon wheels go to jail?
Will: 'Cause they held up a stagecoach.

Matt: Why did the gingerbread boy stay home from school?
Pat: 'Cause he felt crummy.

One night a little boy just wouldn't go to bed. Over and over, he asked his mom for one more drink of water. Finally, his mom said, "I don't want to hear you call 'Mom' one more time!" A little while later, a small voice called out from the boy's room, "Mrs. Taylor, could I have a drink of water?"

Lyle: What's white and can't climb trees?

Kyle: A refrigerator.

I got mugged by six dwarves this morning. Not Happy.

Remy: What do you call a hot dog bun that everyone looks up to?

Isabel: A roll model.

Q: Where did Captain Hook buy his hook?

A: At the secondhand store!

I can't use "beef stew" as a password on my computer. It's not stroganoff.

An odd chick is called egg-centric.

Ed: I don't trust those trees over there.

Ned: Why not?

Ed: They look a little shady.

Charlotte: What do you call a chick going on an ocean voyage?

Rose: An egg-splorer.

City Guy: What do you call a cow that doesn't give milk?

Farmer: An udder failure.

Bob: Why did people think the big cat was lazy?

Rob: He was always lion around.

Nate: Are balloon animals smart?

Jonah: No, they're airheads!

Q: Where do you take a sick horse?

A: To the horse-pital.

Brian: Are those curtains real?

Ryan: No, they're drawn.

Jon: What are twins' favorite fruit?

Ron: Pears!

Mike: What kind of bread has the worst attitude?

Ike: Sourdough.

TONGUE TWiSTERS

Crisp crusts crackle and crunch.

Six slimy snails slid slowly seaward.

Cooks cook cupcakes quickly.

Red lorry, yellow lorry.

Q: What does Mickey Mouse listen to on his way to work?

A: Car-tunes.

Son: Dad, I'm just like Washington, Jefferson, and Lincoln!

Dad: Why's that?

Son: I went down in history.

Hannah: What kind of car does a cat drive?

Deagan: A Fur-rari.

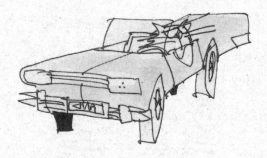

I shook my family tree and a bunch of nuts fell out.

Q: What do you call pasta that has no friends?
A: Ravi-lonely.

Q: Why can't Christmas trees sew?
A: They keep dropping their needles!

Q: How do frogs make breakfast?

A: They use a toad-ster!

Q: What do you call a lamb who dances?

A: A Baaa-lerina.

Is an argument between two vegetarians still called a "beef"?

Q: How much does Santa pay to park his sleigh?

A: Nothing. It's on the house!

My class took a field trip to the soft drink factory. We had a pop quiz afterward.

I have a fear of giants. The doctor says I have fee-fi-phobia.

Max: What's the world's largest onion called?

Jax: A ton-ion.

I love my fingers; I can always count on them.

We should call veterinarians "dogtors."

Someone stole my lamp. Now I'm de-lighted.

Asher: What do you call it when it rains ducks and chickens?

Harper: Fowl weather.

Q: What did Mars say to Saturn?

A: "Give me a ring sometime."

Jason: What do you call a sloppy hippo?

Mason: A hippopota-mess.

Mack: Why did the ancient Egyptians like to shave their heads?

Mike: To be more Pharaoh-dynamic.

Tad: Where do pirates keep their cookies?

Rad: In a cookie *JAAARRRR!*

Q: What do you call five giraffes?

A: A high-five.

Mike: Do you want to talk about infinity?

Deagan: No, I'll never hear the end of it.

Q: How does a snowman get to work?

A: By icicle.

Caden: What do you call a rabbit comedian?

Alsea: A funny bunny.

A funny thing HOPPENED to me on the way over here . . .

If the shoe fits . . . buy another one just like it.

A man rushes into a doctor's office.

Man: Doctor, do you have anything for hiccups?

Doctor: I sure do.

He grabs a glass of ice-cold water and throws it in the man's face.

Doctor: How's that? Did it do the trick?

Man: I don't know. It's for my wife out in the car.
She's the one with the hiccups.

Q: Where do sheep buy their cars?

A: At ewes' car lots.

Office Worker: I hear music coming out of my printer.

Intern: Oh, the paper's jammin' again.

Research says that 70 percent of the population is really dumb. I must be in the other 40 percent.

Q: What do you call a bunch of little dogs with cameras?

A: Pup-arazzi.

Bill: What does a baby computer call its father?

Phil: "Data!"

Q: What do you call one of Santa's helpers who is rich?

A: Welfy.

Hannah: What do cows read at breakfast?

Bo: The mooospaper.

Bill: Should you have your entire family for Thanksgiving dinner?

Jill: No, we'll just stick with turkey.

Caden: Did you hear about the actor who fell through the floorboards?

Braedon: No, what happened?

Caden: Nothing. He was just going through a stage.

Q: What do you call a sleepy fruit?

A: A nap-ricot.

Max: What do you call an elephant in a VW Bug?

Alsea: Stuck.

Farm Kid: What does it mean when you find a horseshoe?

City Kid: Some poor horse is walking around in his socks!

Q: What do you call a snowman's temper tantrum?

A: A meltdown.

Q: What's a snowman's favorite game?

A: Ice Spy.

Connor: If athletes get athlete's foot, what do astronauts get?

Kylie: Missile toe.

Q: What does a farmer wear in the fall?

A: A har-vest!

Ed: What do you get when you drop a pumpkin
from the sixth floor?

Ned: A squash.

Pat: Why are skeletons so calm?

Matt: Because nothing gets under their skin.

Q: Who leads all the apples to the bakery?

A: The Pie Piper.

Kylie: What do you call it when a tree goes on vacation?

Harper: Paid leaf.

Q: What's a chick's favorite drink?

A: Peepsi-Cola.

Q: What did Obi-Wan Kenobi say in the restaurant?

A: "Use the fork, Luke."

Q: Why did the Easter egg hide?

A: He was a little chicken.

Logan: Why is your dog staring at me?

Rogan: Maybe 'cause you're eating out of his bowl.

Q: What do librarians take with them when they go fishing?

A: Bookworms.

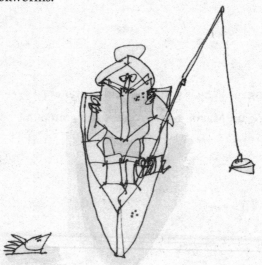

Saw an ad for an old radio for just a dollar—said the volume was stuck on high. I said to myself, *I can't turn that down.*

Q: What happened to the chick that acted up in school?

A: She was egg-spelled.

Chloe: Why is your fish wearing a soccer uniform?

Connor: He's my goal-fish.

Pat: What do you call an egg that's always playing tricks on people?

Matt: A practical yolker.

Q: What do you call a doe caught in a storm?

A: A rain-deer.

Lyle: Why is it hard to have a conversation with a goat?

Kyle: 'Cause they're always butting in.

Oh, that reminds me of a story . . .

Jack: Why did the rooster cross the road?

Zach: He needed to cock-a-doodle-do something.

Sal: Why did no one play games with the big cat on the ark?

Hal: 'Cause they knew he was a cheetah.

Q: Why did the duck fall down on the sidewalk?

A: It tripped over a quack.

Q: What do you take before every meal?

A: A seat.

Q: How does the sky pay its bill?

A: With a rain check.

Randy: Never tell a burrito a secret.

Andy: Why not?

Randy: They might just spill the beans.

I ran into twin octopuses—they were i-tentacle!

Q: What falls down in the winter but never gets hurt?

A: Snow.

I tried working for a pool maintenance company, but the job was too draining.

Q: What did one volcano say to the other volcano?
A: "I lava you!"

Joe: What time is it when the clock strikes thirteen?
Bo: Time to get a new clock.

Bill: What do you get when you cross a pie with a snake?

Will: A pie-thon.

Ryan: What kind of dog is the best artist?

Brian: A labra-doodler.

Q: What kind of motorcycle does Santa ride?

A: A Holly-Davidson.

Ron: Who's a penguin's favorite aunt?

Jon: Aunt Arctica!

I'm so good at sleeping, I can do it with my eyes closed.

Caden: Who loves hamburgers, fries, and ants?

Alsea: Ronald McAardvark!

Doctor: Have you been sleeping with an open window like I suggested?

Patient: Yes.

Doctor: So, is the congestion gone?

Patient: No. So far, the only things that are gone are my laptop and my flat-screen TV.

Brian: When I drink coffee, I can't sleep.

Ryan: Wow, I have just the opposite problem.

Brian: Really?

Ryan: Yeah. When I sleep, I can't drink coffee.

Q: How do mountains stay warm in the winter?

A: They wear their snowcaps.

Q: What is a little dog's favorite dessert?

A: Pup-cakes!

I was going to tell you the fruit-drink joke, but I forgot the punch line.

I didn't like my beard at first. Then it grew on me.

Len: I just got a job at a bakery.

Ben: Why's that?

Len: I kneaded the dough.

I wish more people were fluent in silence.

TONGUE TWISTERS

Sheena leads, Sheila needs.

Tie twine to three tree twigs.

I wish to wash my Irish wristwatch.

Thin grippy, thick slippery.

Q: What do you get when you cross a great white shark with a computer?

A: A mega-bite.

Be kind to your dentist—after all, he has fillings too.

What are you doing with that badge?
You're a pumpkin!

I'm a security gourd.

Q: Why are frogs always so happy?

A: They eat whatever bugs them.

I dig, you dig, he digs, she digs, they dig. Not a great poem, but it's really deep.

Did you hear about the astronaut who hated tight places? He just needed a little space.

I'm going out for some fresh air.

Q: What does a nosy pepper do?

A: Gets jalapeño business.

Q: What is an astronaut's favorite part of a computer?

A: The space bar.

That scary French bakery gives me the crepes.

Q: Why did the Oreo go to the dentist?

A: He lost his filling.

I got my wife a refrigerator for her birthday. I can't wait to see her face light up when she opens it.

The rotation of the earth really makes my day.

Asher: Why did the nurse bring a red pen to work?

Harper: In case she needed to draw blood.

Q: What do you call a train carrying bubble gum?

A: A chew-chew train.

Q: Why should you never tell a secret to a pig?

A: It's bound to squeal.

Q: What's in the middle of a gummy bear?
A: A jelly button.

Q: What do you call a guy who used to dig ditches?
A: Doug.

Escalators don't break down—they just turn into stairs.

Rob: How did Benjamin Franklin feel when
he discovered electricity?
Bob: He was shocked!

Bob: Why are you hitting that cake with a hammer?

Rob: It's a pound cake.

Bill: Why did the whale cross the ocean?

Will: To get to the other tide.

Q: What does a bee use to cut wood?

A: A buzz saw.

Q: Who's the smartest bird in the world?

A: Owlbert Einstein.

Q: What state has the most cats and dogs?

A: Pets-ylvania.

Teacher: If chickens get up when the rooster crows, when do ducks get up?

Devon: At the quack of dawn.

Knock, knock.

Who's there?

Amos.

Amos who?

A mosquito just bit me.

Q: What kind of car does an egg own?

A: A Yolkswagen!

Dan: What happened when the strawberry crossed
the road?

Jan: There was a traffic jam.

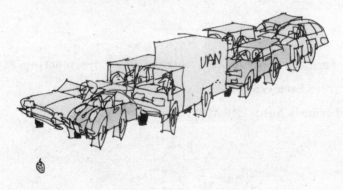

Q: What do you call a cow that's run out of milk?

A: A Milk Dud.

I just took a picture of a wheat field. It came out a little grainy.

Caden: Does your dog have a license?

Max: No, I never let him drive.

Farmer's Son: One cow, two cows, three cows, four cows . . .

Farmer: What are you doing?

Farmer's Son: Cownting.

Q: What kind of lions are the best swimmers?

A: Sea lions.

I'm starting a chicken-feed business. I'm just waiting for some seed money.

A truck loaded with vapor rub overturned on the freeway yesterday. Oddly enough, there was no congestion for eight hours.

I do all my addition in my head. It's the thought that counts.

Q: What time is it when ten lions are chasing you?

A: Ten after one.

Q: What kind of fish only appears at night?

A: A starfish.

Q: What do you get when you cross a chick with a
   Slinky?

A: A spring chicken.

Warning! Don't spell *Part A* backwards. It's a trap.

Most people don't keep their New Year's resolutions. They go in one year and out the other.

Q: What do you call a newborn female plant?

A: A Girl Sprout.

Knock, knock.

Who's there?

Spell.

Spell who?

Okay, W-H-O.

Q: What did the hot fudge say to the ice cream?

A: "Don't worry, I've got you covered."

Bo: They're not going to make yardsticks any longer.

Iris: Really?

Bo: Yeah, they're going to keep them at three feet.

My recliner and I go way back.

Don: What do you call a string bean that got old?

Jon: A has-bean.

Q: **What do you call a girl who's in the middle of a tennis court?**

A: Annette.

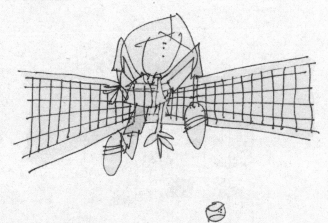

Q: **What state has the smallest soft drinks?**

A: Mini-soda.

I've started telling everyone about the benefits of eating dried grapes. It's all about raisin awareness.

Rick: How do you get a farmer's daughter to fall for you?

Nick: A tractor.

A little boy was going to bed during a loud thunderstorm. He sat up and asked his mom, "Will you sleep with me tonight?"

"I can't," she answered. "I have to sleep with Daddy."

"So, he's scared too?" the boy said. "The big baby."

Bo: I'm sorry I gave you a bad haircut.

Joe: That's okay; I'll keep it under my hat.

I lost my voice. I'm sorry, I can't talk about it.

Ed: Why did the horse talk with his mouth full?
Ted: Because he had bad stable manners.

Mary: Why can't you ever call the zoo?
Shari: 'Cause the lion is always busy.

Mike: Why did the music students get in trouble?

Ike: They were caught passing notes!

Crushing soft drink cans can be soda pressing.

Jason: What kind of fish fixes your grand piano?

Mason: A piano tuna.

Bill: I accidently plugged my electric blanket into the toaster last night.

Will: What happened?

Bill: I spent all night popping out of bed.

Tim: Why was the ice cream lonely?

Jim: Because the banana split.

Q: What bet can never be won?

A: The alphabet.

Q: What did the hot dog say to the tomato?

A: "Let's get together soon so we can ketchup."

Q: What does a farmer say when he starts a party?

A: "Lettuce turnip the beet!"

Knock, knock.

Who's there?

Baron.

Baron who?

Baron mind who you're talking to.

Knock, knock.

Who's there?

Avery.

Avery who?

Avery time I come over to your house we go through this!

Knock, knock.

Who's there?

Ben.

Ben who?

Ben knocking on this door all morning!

Knock, knock.

Who's there?

Canoe.

Canoe who?

Canoe come out and play?

This cheese saved the entire world! It was legend dairy.

Ben: What do you call a clumsy letter?
Len: A bumble *B*.

Macy: Why did the vegetable boat sink?
Lacey: It was full of leeks!

Who brought all these leeks?!?

Teacher: Name five things that contain milk.

Kid: Butter, cheese, ice cream, and . . . two cows!

Mary: Why did you stop dating the seismologist?

Shari: He was too quick to find faults.

Is a kid who's refusing to nap resisting a rest?

Got a job as a historian but realized there was no future in it.

Two guys went to the movies together. One brought his dog. The friend was amazed because the dog seemed to follow the story, laughing in all the right places and getting really quiet at the sad parts. After the movie, the friend couldn't stand it anymore. He said, "This is amazing. Your dog seemed to actually enjoy the movie!"

"Yeah, I was shocked," the dog owner said. "He hated the book."

Q: Why didn't the baseball player score any points?

A: He kept running home.

Ben: Why did the opera singer need a ladder?

Jen: She wanted to reach the high notes.

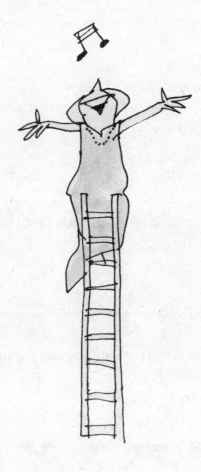

I used to wear winter gloves all the time. Now I only wear them intermittenly.

Pat: What do you call a can opener that won't work?

Matt: A can't opener.

Exaggerations went up by a million percent last month.

My friend invented an invisible airplane, but I can't see it taking off.

Bill: What do you call 30 pandas playing musical chairs?

Jill: Panda-monium.

Customer: This bread you sold me is full of holes!

Baker: What do you expect? It's hole wheat bread.

Q: What do you call a Frenchman wearing sandals?
A: Phillipe Phillop.

When you were growing up, how small was your house?

It was so small I had to go outside to change my mind.

It was so small the mice were hunchbacked.

When I stuck the key in the front door, I broke the back window.

When I turned around, I was next door.

I ordered a large pizza and had to eat it outside.

When I stepped through the front door, I was in the backyard.

When I dropped a tissue, I got wall-to-wall carpeting.

When we ate in the kitchen, our elbows were in the living room.

TONGUE TWISTERS

Can you scan a can the way a can scanner can?

Betty and Bob brought back blue balloons from the big bazaar.

Rubber baby buggy bumpers.

Knock, knock.

Who's there?

Snow.

Snow who?

Snow fun to do my homework.

I love jokes about eyes. The cornea the better.

To the guy who stole my glasses: I will find you. I have contacts.

A guy tried to sell me a mirror, but I knew it was a scam. I could see right through it.

Knock, knock.

Who's there?

Kayak.

Kayak who?

Kayak with you about something?

I was driving my bread car when it caught on fire. Now it's toast.

I swapped our bed for a trampoline. My wife hit the roof.

Q: How do meteorologists go up a mountain?

A: They climate.

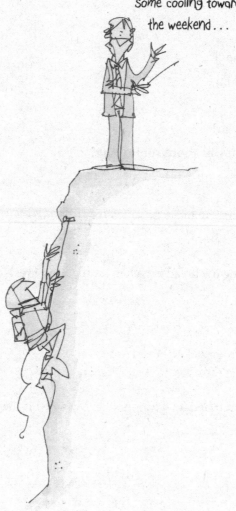

Two guys fell down a hole. One said, "Wow, it's dark in here, isn't it?"

The other one answered, "I don't know; I can't see."

Kid: Dad, can you tell me what a solar eclipse is?

Dad: No sun.

Q: Which one of Santa's reindeer has bad manners?

A: Rude-olph.

I got a compliment on my driving. Someone left a note on my windshield that said, "Parking fine."

Q: **Why did the kid drop veggies all over his map of the world?**

A: He wanted peas on earth.

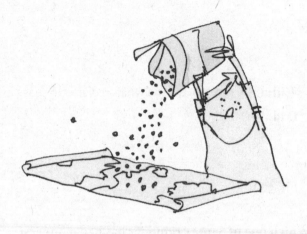

Q: **What yummy snack is always speaking?**

A: A talk-o.

Q: What does the cat like on her toast in the morning?

A: Orange meow-malade.

Q: What's a cat's favorite brand of diapers?

A: Pam-purrs.

Two boys went with their parents to a wedding. As they watched the proceedings, one turned to the other and whispered, "How many wives can a man have?"

"I don't know, why?"

"So far I've counted sixteen."

"Sixteen?"

"Yeah—four better, four worse, four richer, four poorer."

Flo: Thanks for hooking up my dog and taking him for a walk.

Joe: No problem. It's the leash I could do.

Q: What superhero likes freshly pressed clothes?
A: Iron Man.

Q: What's a kitten's favorite subject in school?

A: Mewsic.

Knock, knock.

Who's there?

Cattle.

Cattle who?

Cattle purr if you pet her.

Terry: How did Mickey Mouse save Minnie from drowning?

Jerry: He gave her mouse-to-mouse resuscitation.

Asher: What do you get when you cross a cocker spaniel, a poodle, and a rooster?

Harper: A cocker-poodle-do.

Andy: Where did the Wright Brothers' cat invent the airplane?

Randy: Kitty Hawk.

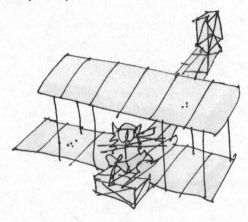

Q: What do a boat captain and a hatmaker have in common?

A: They're both concerned with capsizing.

Q: Where do young chickens go on vacation?

A: Chickago.

Jonny: Mom, can I go out and play?

Mom: What? With those holes in your sock?

Jonny: No, with the kids next door.

Q: What's a cheerleader's favorite cereal?

A: Cheerios!

Q: What's a turkey's favorite holiday?

A: Feather's Day.

Q: Why did the builder hire chickens to work on his crew?

A: They were cheep labor.

Q: What do you call a company that makes just average stuff?

A: A satis-factory.

Q: What does the Easter Bunny grow in his garden?

A: Eggplants.

Q: Why does the chef always laugh while he's making breakfast?

A: Because the egg always cracks a yolk.

Q: Why was the calendar so jumpy?

A: It was a leap year.

Q: Where do penguins go to see movies?

A: The dive-in.

Q: Why was the grizzly turned away from the restaurant?

A: Because there were no bear feet allowed.

Q: Why did the socks move to the fruit orchard?

A: They liked living in pears.

Q: What does a buffalo wear to the pool?

A: Bison-glasses.

Q: Where do cats wait to pay their bills?

A: In the fee line.

Teacher: How long does it take to make butter?

Farm Boy: An echurnity!

I told my doctor I broke my arm in two places. He told me to avoid those places.

Teacher: What kind of nut has no shell?
Benjamin: A doughnut!

I understand how cars work, but airplanes are way over my head.

The best time on a clock is 6:30, hands down.

Kid: Mom, there's going to be a small PTA meeting tonight.
Mom: What do you mean "small"?
Kid: Just you, me, and the principal.

Q: What kind of cheese likes to shoot hoops?

A: *Swish* cheese.

You can take a horse to water, but a pencil must be led.

Len: Why should you always bring chips to a party?

Ben: In queso emergency.

Q: How do monkeys stay in shape?

A: They go to the jungle gym.

Chloe: What's a frog's favorite restaurant?

Kylie: IHOP.

Just went to an outdoor wedding and it rained the entire time. The whole thing was in tents.

Q: What kind of tree can fit in your hand?

A: A palm tree.

Ben: A king had three goblets. Two were full and one was half full. What was the king's name?

Len: I give up.

Ben: Phillip the Third!

Q: What is a computer tech's favorite dessert?

A: Apple pie à la modem.

Q: What do you call a knight who's afraid to fight?

A: Sir Render.

Man: I'd like to place a call to Wenatchee, Washington.

Operator: Can you spell that?

Man: If I could spell it, I'd write a letter.

People want the front of the bus, the back of the church, and the center of attention.

TONGUE TWISTERS

Silly Sally swiftly shooed seven silly sheep.

Six sick hicks nick six slick bricks with picks and sticks.

Round the rough and rugged rock, the ragged rascal rudely ran.

Ed had edited it.

She sells seashells at the seashore. So, if she sells shells at the seashore, I'm sure she sells seashore shells.

Knock, knock.

Who's there?

Iris.

Iris who?

Iris-eived a package in the mail. Was it from you?

Knock, knock.

Who's there?

Rita.

Rita who?

Rita good book lately?

Knock, knock.

Who's there?

Ira.

Ira who?

Ira-member you; do you remember me?

Today we're going to learn
how to make a fire out of doors.

Great, but where will we get
all the doors?

Knock, knock.

Who's there?

Edith.

Edith who?

Edith thick juithy burger for me, will ya?

Knock, knock.

Who's there?

Alex.

Alex who?

Alex some more root beer, please.

Knock, knock.

Who's there?

Isabel.

Isabel who?

Isabel working or should I just keep knocking?

A city guy was renting a horse for the day. The wrangler asked, "Do you want a saddle horn?"

"Naw," the city guy answered. "I figure I won't run into much traffic."

Customer: What's that fly doing in my alphabet soup?

Waiter: Trying to learn to read?

Christy: I keep thinking today is Monday.

Misty: Today *is* Monday.

Christy: I know, that's why I keep thinking it.

Mom: Why do you keep burping?

Max: I had belchin' waffles for breakfast.

Teacher: Harper, please use the word *column* in a sentence.

Harper: When I want to talk to my friend, I column up on the phone.

Patient: Doc, to be honest, I don't feel any better since our last visit.

Doctor: Did you follow the directions on the bottle of medicine I gave you?

Patient: Sure did. The bottle said, "Keep tightly closed."

BACKWARD JOKES

Backward jokes give the answer first, then the question. Here's an example:

The answer is, *A paradox*.
The question is, *What do you call two surgeons walking down the hall?*

Answer: Rampage.

Question: What do they call a sheet in the LA football team's playbook?

Answer: Lumberjack.

Question: What do you call it when someone steals your lumber?

Answer: Semiconductor.

Question: What do you call a part-time orchestra leader?

Answer: Europe.

Question: What does the umpire say when it's your turn to bat?

Answer: Protein.

Question: What do you call a teenager who plays a sport for money?

Answer: Padlock.

Question: How does a frog keep his home secure?

Answer: Plymouth Rock.

Question: What kind of music did the pilgrims listen to?

Answer: Chicken coop.

Question: What does a chicken drive if the chicken sedan
isn't available?

Answer: Ocean liner.

Question: What's another name for sand?

Answer: Polygon.

Question: What do you say when your parrot flies away?

Answer: A pup tent.

Question: What does Lassie take with her on campouts?

Answer: Submission.

Question: What do you call it when a submarine goes on a
trip?

Answer: Babysitter.

Question: What's another name for a high chair?

Liam: Mom, you know that vase that's been handed
down from generation to generation?

Mom: Yes.

Liam: Well, this generation dropped it.

Cop: You look like you were pushing 60.

Phyllis: How rude! I'm only 45.

Chef: I've been cooking for 25 years.

Diner: Then I guess my order is almost ready.

Kyle: Dad, I can't get the car started. I think it's flooded.

Dad: Where is it?

Kyle: In the swimming pool.

I sold my vacuum cleaner the other day. All it was doing was collecting dust.

Man: Doctor, you've got to help me! I'm convinced I'm a poodle.

Psychiatrist: How long have you felt like this?

Man: Ever since I was a puppy.

Dad: Well, son, you've got one thing in your favor.

Jon: What's that?

Dad: With this report card, you couldn't possibly be cheating.

Two businessmen sit down in a roadside diner.

Mac: I'd like a cup of coffee.

Jack: Me too, and make sure it's in a clean cup.

The waitress comes back a couple minutes later with their coffee.

Waitress: Okay, which one of you ordered a clean cup?

Q: What's a cop's favorite board game?

A: Monopolice.

Asher: What's a karate champion's favorite dish?

Harper: Kung food.

Q: What kind of key opens a banana?

A: A mon-key.

Q: What Olympic race is never run?

A: The swimming race.

Max: Why did you get that Good Drivers Award?

Caden: Because I was wreck-less.

Bo: What did the dog say after a long day at work?

Iris: "Wow, today was ruff."

Ron: My dad's never done a day's work in his life.

Jon: Why not?

Ron: He's a night watchman.

Randy: What does a chicken need to finish a marathon?

Andy: Hen-durance.

Will: Why couldn't the chicken find her eggs?

Jill: 'Cause she mislaid them.

Ed: What do chickens serve at birthday parties?

Ned: Coop-cakes.

Jason: What time do chickens go to bed?

Mason: At half past hen.

Did you hear that the invisible man married the invisible woman? Their kids aren't much to look at either.

Q: What flower rules the garden?

A: The dande-lion.

Q: What do baby kangaroos wear?

A: Jumpsuits.

I have a phobia of German sausage. I fear the wurst.

Q: What do snakes take for a cold?

A: Anti-hiss-tamines.

My fear of moving stairs is escalating.

Q: Why did the laptop get glasses?
A: To improve his web-sight.

Remy: I fell off my horse in the barn this afternoon.
Charlotte: Are you okay?
Remy: Yeah, the doctor said my condition was
stable.

Deagan: Left my glasses at home yesterday. Guess who I
bumped into?
Hannah: Who?
Deagan: Everyone!

Mom: Brandon, what was that?
Brandon: My shirt fell on the ground.
Mom: Why was it so loud?
Brandon: I was in it.

Q: How do ducks celebrate the Fourth of July?

A: With firequackers.

Q: Who's the pig's favorite movie star?

A: Kevin Bacon.

Q: Where do cows, chickens, and horses get their medications?

A: At Old MacDonald's Farmacy.

Q: What do you call a helicopter with a skunk inside?

A: A smelly-copter.

Q: What do you get when you cross a pig with a newscaster?

A: An oinkerman.

And now here's the news...

Son: Dad, I want to drive a tank in the army.

Dad: Well, I won't stand in your way.

Principal: Why were you acting up in orchestra class?

Connor: I just didn't know how to conduct myself.

Q: What has 100 legs and says, "Ho, ho, ho"?

A: A Santa-pede.

Knock, knock.

Who's there?

Comma.

Comma who?

Comma little closer and see for yourself.

Knock, knock.

Who's there?

Harmony.

Harmony who?

Harmony times do I need to knock on the door before you let me in?

Q: What do you get when you cross a bunny with a flatbread sandwich?

A: Pita Rabbit.

I lost another audiobook. Now I'll never hear the end of it.

Terry: Why did you get fired from the computer keyboard factory?

Jerry: I wasn't putting in enough shifts.

Did you hear my new song about tortillas? Actually, it's more of a wrap.

Chloe: What rock group has four guys who don't sing?

Kylie: Mount Rushmore.

A snail was riding on a turtle's back when it crashed into another turtle. The cop asked the snail what happened. He said, "I don't know; it all happened so fast!"

I ordered a chicken and an egg off the internet just to see which came first.

We're collecting vegetable jokes. If you have any, lettuce know.

Why did you lose your job?

> Barber: Kept taking shortcuts.

> Doctor: Was short on patients.

> Taxi Driver: Kept driving my customers away.

Moving-Van Driver: Got carried away with my work.

Dentist: I was always looking down in the mouth.

Coin-Mint Worker: I stopped making cents.

Giraffe Feeder at the Zoo: I wasn't up to the task.

Worker in an Origami Store: I worked there until it folded.

Q: What do you call a snail who joins the Navy?

A: A snailor.

Q: Where do pig Eskimos live?
A: In pigloos!

Q: What kind of tree does a math teacher climb?
A: A geometry!

I went on a once-in-a-lifetime vacation. Never again.

Bo: Which is faster: hot or cold?
Iris: Hot, because you can always catch a cold.

Time is what keeps things from happening all at once.

Q: Why did the pony get sent to the principal's office?

A: He was horsing around.

Isabel: Why did the bee get married?

Rose: Because he found his honey!

When tempted to fight fire with fire, remember that the fire department usually uses water.

Teacher: Steven, how far were you from the right answer?

Steven: Just two seats.

Q: What's brown, hairy, and wears sunglasses?

A: A coconut on vacation.

Q: Why doesn't the farmer's dog like his sheep jokes?

A: Because he's herd them all.

Q: What is a tornado's favorite game to play?

A: Twister!

Q: What's green and wears a cape?

A: Super Pickle.

Q: What did the big flower say to the little flower?

A: "Hi, bud."

Braedon: What does bread do on the weekends?

Caden: Just loafs around.

Asher: What does a flower say when it's teasing?

Harper: "I'm just pollen your leg."

Max: What do you call a flamingo at the North
         Pole?

Alsea: Lost.

Ava: How do you fix a broken tomato?

Rowan: With tomato paste.

Knock, knock.

   Who's there?

Chicken.

   Chicken who?

Chicken your pockets; your keys might be in there.

Man: Doctor, I'm convinced I'm an elevator!

Psychiatrist: Can you come in to see me immediately?

Man: I can't; I don't stop at your floor!

Two artists had an art contest. It ended in a draw.

Donny: Where do fish sleep?

Ronny: In a riverbed.

I tried to sue the airline for losing my luggage. I lost my case.

Tad: Why did the boy bring a ladder to the football game?

Rad: He heard the Giants were playing.

Do you think Earth makes fun of other planets for having no life?

Boss: Can you come in on Saturday? I really need you.

Steven: Sure, but I might be a little late. Buses are slow on the weekend.

Boss: What time will you get here?

Steven: Monday.

Sal: Why did the two fours skip dinner?

Hal: They already eight!

Jack: Why did the vegetable gardener quit her job?

Zach: Her celery wasn't high enough.

Brian: A year ago, my doctor told me I was losing my hearing.

Ryan: What happened?

Brian: I haven't heard from him since.

Lyle: What happened to you?

Kyle: I broke my leg raking leaves.

Lyle: How did you do that?

Kyle: Fell out of the tree.

Q: What did the dalmatian say after he ate his dinner?

A: "That hit the spot."

Hannah: Why are you putting that cake in the freezer?

Deagan: The recipe says to ice it after baking.

Mason: Why shouldn't you talk to a broken pencil?

Jason: It's pointless.

Bob: How do you make more room for pigs on a farm?

Rob: Build a sty-scraper.

Charlotte: Where do polar bears vote?

Remy: The North Poll.

Patient: Doctor, I'm convinced I'm an alligator!

Doctor: Well, can you come in next week? Right now, I'm swamped.

Knock, knock.

Who's there?

An author.

An author who?

An author joke like this and I'm outta here!

EMILY BIDDLE RETURNS

Book Titles

Digging into Ancient History by R. K. Ology

It's Your Choice! by Howard U. Lykett

I'm Tired of Schoolwork! by Anita Vacation

Communicating with Cows by I. Ken Moo

Would You Like a Million Dollars? by Sherwood B. Nice

Learn How to Dance by Tristin Shout

I'm Just Kidding! by Shirley U. Jest

Discovering Dinosaurs by Tara Dacktill

Raising Pigs, Goats, and Cattle by Iona Farm

Getting Close to Bees by I. Ben Stung

More Book Titles

The World's Easiest Diet by M. T. Cupboards

How I Crossed the Sahara by Rhoda Camel

Working at the Gas Station by Phil R. Upp

Ham on Rye by Della Catessen

Who Saw Him Go? by Wendy Leave

101 Recipes by R. U. Hungry

Simple Household Fixes by Andy Mann

The Laser Battle by Ray Gunn

Awake All Night by Constance Noring

Exploring the South Pole by Anne Arctic

SANDY SILVERTHORNE

has been writing and illustrating books since 1988, with nearly one million copies sold. He is the award-winning creator of the Great Bible Adventure children's series, several joke books for kids, *The Best Worst Dad Jokes*, and *Kids' Big Questions for God*. Sandy has worked as a cartoonist, author, illustrator, actor, pastor, speaker, and comedian. Apparently, it's hard for him to focus.

CONNECT WITH SANDY

www.SandySilverthorneBooks.com

@SandySilverthornesPage

@SandSilver

@SandySilverthorne